Ministry of Housing and Local Government

Historic towns **Preservation and change**

London Her Majesty's Stationery Office 1967

VCE
HIS

Foreword

by the Minister of Housing and Local Government

This book, produced by the Ministry of Housing and Local Government, is about an aspect of town planning that is now receiving more and more attention : the kind of planning which is needed in order to preserve, in a positive way, the good things our towns already possess.

It is concerned not only with single old buildings, but also with the general visual qualities of historic towns, for the traditional English townscape is often just as enjoyable and as much worth preserving as the English countryside. The fact that people come from all over the world to visit our historic towns makes it plain that they are one of our most important cultural and economic assets.

There is of course much in our towns that needs to be changed, and there is no reason why preservation should prevent desirable change. But changes which destroy something good are only desirable if they produce something which is clearly better. The book suggests that the surest way to avoid a conflict between the old and the new is to plan preservation and change together, keeping what ought to be kept, and ensuring that what new development there is goes well with it.

This is not a technical planning handbook. It is written primarily for laymen. Its aim is to focus attention on a problem which concerns us all, and to promote a common understanding among all those who are responsible in different ways for the future of our towns — members of local councils and their staffs, architects, planners, builders, property-owners, traders, and, most important of all, the ordinary citizen.

Contents

List of illustrations

Acknowledgments

Thanks are due to the following for permission to reproduce copyright photographs :
Figures
6   *Architects' Journal*
8 and 49   The *Guardian* newspaper
47 and 48   The Civic Trust
50   Beacon Studios, Brecon
51 and 55   The Greater London Council
52 and 53   Blaby Rural District Council
64   Thomas—Photos, Oxford
The rest of the photographs are crown copyright, the majority having been specially
taken by photographers of the National Monuments Record

1

Changing towns

1

2

The towns of England are as varied, interesting, and handsome as its countryside. They are what they are because generation after generation has brought its own style, its own skill, its own eye, to the never-ending task of keeping them up-to-date.

They have been subject to continual change, especially in the town centres where commercial, cultural and social activities meet. Here renewal tends to accelerate and spread as towns grow and the expanding population makes further demands on the centres for trade, entertainment and public affairs. In the course of time the whole centre may be rebuilt. This has happened not once, but repeatedly, in some of our ancient cities. The remains of Roman Chichester, for example, now lie some five feet below the present surface, after centuries of building and rebuilding.

But for the most part change has been gradual and piecemeal. Towns grew and new estates were laid out on their fringes, but until recent times comparatively little large-scale redevelopment took place within them. Rebuilding was occasional and sporadic, the new buildings usually being on a scale with the old, so that the effect on the general aspect of a town would be gradual.

We owe much to this slow, piecemeal process of renewal. It has given us some of the most beautiful streets in the world and the richly varied texture, the 'visible history', that is characteristic of so many of our older towns (1, 2, 3).

Today it is different. The tempo has quickened, and most towns are changing more rapidly than ever before in response to the needs of a fast-growing population with rising standards of living, and under the impact of motor traffic. Since 1900, the population of England and Wales has grown by some fifteen million ; and today

1   High Street, Lewes

2   Castle Street, Farnham

3   The High, Oxford

nine people in every ten live in towns. The volume of urban development now in progress far exceeds anything hitherto attained. At the present rate we could re-build every town in the country over again in fifty years, and the rate is still increasing.

From the invention of the wheel until about the beginning of this century town traffic remained essentially the same ; people on foot and horseback, and horse-drawn vehicles. The flood of motor traffic that has burst upon us since then has made unprecedented demands upon our towns, for more and wider thorough-fares, for greater circulation space, for the separation of walkers from vehicles, and for extensive parking places. It has made itself felt in other ways — in noise, fumes and visual intrusion. All in all, it is the most disruptive force that has ever assailed our towns in peacetime.

The twentieth century has brought count-less benefits to town-dwellers, but it has done much damage to their towns. Many buildings of grace and distinction have been demolished (4, 5, 6).

4   The Euston Arch

5   3 St. James' Street South, Bath

6   Interior of the Coal Exchange, City of London

7

8

Others have been ruined almost as effectively by the destruction of their environment (7). Old streets and terraces have lost their architectural unity through insensitive 'infilling'. The historic centres of old towns have been torn apart by massive schemes of comprehensive re-development (8). Whatever the reasons for these losses, they are all irrevocable.

The scale of operations is now greater than before. Larger areas are taken for redevelopment and a single new building may replace half a dozen old ones (9, 10a, 10b).

The variegated, fine-grained texture created by occasional rebuilding in the past is being superseded by larger units of standardised types, for the new building forms and the materials of which they are made are ubiquitous; steel, concrete and glass are now used the world over. Traditional designs and local materials are seldom employed. As a result, the newly-developed parts of towns everywhere begin to look alike.

What should be done? We cannot bring change to a halt; that was not the way of earlier generations, and there is much in towns today that must be changed. But the forces of change are now so powerful that they need to be controlled and directed. They may be economically as well as visually destructive. Consider how much wealth is brought to, for instance, Oxford or Bath (to say nothing of Venice or Paris) by visitors who like them as they are. Clearly we could not simply 'let rip' saving only the great cathedrals and other masterpieces of the past and abandoning all else. That would mean the loss of the better part of our heritage as well as the worst, and of all that is familiar and rooted in the past. We should have to face the possibility that every town *would* be largely rebuilt within fifty years; that all the familiar features of towns as we know them today would be obliterated, not by the slow attrition of centuries, but in a lifetime.

The alternative is to take stock now, before it is too late, and decide what are the things we want to keep; then to see how this can be done without preventing desirable change. We may in the process discover possibilities of restoring assets which have been neglected in the past, and of making improvements that have never yet been thought of. First, what do we want to keep?

7   The Black Swan, Peaseholme Street, York

8   Worcester

9   High Street, Guildford

10a b Park Lane, London, before and after redevelopment

2

What to preserve?

It is often said that England's most important contribution to the visual arts is her architecture. This embraces not only the great country houses, but, equally important if less spectacular, our many ancient towns and villages. They contain a wealth of buildings of great interest and present an immense variety of plan, periods, materials and styles.

Several towns like Chichester and Chester retain the street plans of their Roman foundation although no complete buildings of that period survive. Other towns are of medieval foundation and have grown up on strategic hill-tops, at river crossings or as market centres. One at least, Winchelsea, was a 'new town' of the reign of Edward I with a grid-iron street plan that has survived (12). Great Shambles at York (11) and Mercery Lane at Canterbury (13) are good examples of narrow medieval streets with overhanging upper storeys.

12

13

11   Great Shambles, York

12   Winchelsea

13   Mercery Lane, Canterbury

14

15

The great prosperity of the woollen industry in the fifteenth century led to extensive building in many towns such as Lavenham and Cranbrook. Many timber-framed buildings and hall houses with elaborate roof timbering survive from this period (14). In the seventeenth century the use of brick and stone in preference to timber became more general, and most old towns can show examples of the style associated with Sir Christopher Wren and his time (15). By the eighteenth century brick and stone predominated, although in many cases they were used only to provide a new street elevation to an older building. Sometimes even the old fronts were retained, with the addition of new features such as eaves, cornices, sash windows and hipped roofs instead of gables. But in many towns which were the centres of agricultural prosperity rebuilding was on a more generous scale, and it is at this period that the formal group of houses with uniform facades — a terrace, square or crescent — makes its appearance. The supreme example is the development of the great city of Bath in the eighteenth century (16). With the growth of resorts like Brighton and Cheltenham in the early nineteenth century, this form of construction became more common, often with stucco instead of stone for the street elevations. Most towns have one or more groups of this kind to show. The Georgian terrace, in the common form in which one sees it in London and Liverpool and a hundred other places, is one of the most distinctive and civilised inventions of English culture (17).

14 The Guildhall, Lavenham

15 Pallent House, Chichester

16 Queen Square, Bath

17 Doughty Street, London

The growing momentum of the Industrial Revolution in this period has also left its mark in the cloth mills, breweries and other early industrial buildings which survive, many of them designed with the same elegance as domestic buildings of this time (18).

With the beginning of Queen Victoria's reign styles became more diverse. Until recently Victorian buildings have been little valued by the general public, partly because there are so many of them. But it is now commonly realised that the best examples of Victorian architecture are as important and as much a part of the national heritage as those of earlier periods (20, 21). Some buildings were important for the use of new materials or forms of construction. Some whole suburbs, laid out under a guiding plan, such as Port Sunlight at Bebington in Cheshire (19), can rank with the best of any period.

18   Cressbrook Mill, Derbyshire

19   Port Sunlight, Cheshire

20   St. Pancras Hotel, London

21   St. Philip Neri Church, Arundel

The design of buildings varies not only from period to period, but also from place to place. It is this regional variation in styles and materials, more than anything else, that gives towns their particular character and identity.

When houses were everywhere built with timber frames, their decoration varied from place to place. In the counties of the West Midlands from Cheshire through Warwickshire and round to Herefordshire the elevations were often decorated with the elaborate patterns of timbering that characterise the 'black and white' houses of the region (22).

In East Anglia contemporary houses were almost always plastered and in some cases adorned with delicate patterns of pargetting (23). When timber-framed houses were later reinforced against the weather, in Kent the builders favoured weather-boarding, in Sussex and Surrey weather-tiles (24), in Devonshire slates (25).

22   The Feathers Hotel, Ludlow

23   Sparrow's House, Ipswich

22

23

24

Where stone was available its use for walls and roofs produced local styles which varied little between the sixteenth and the nineteenth centuries, as in the Cotswolds. But the colour of the local product changed from region to region, from the golden ham stone of Somerset and Dorset to North Oxfordshire iron stone and the very dark stones of the north of England. Other materials show an equal variety of colour and texture ; for example the rich red bricks of the southern counties, lighter vitreous bricks and 'blue' bricks. Flints or cobbles were extensively used in seaside areas and chalklands, sometimes set with their rounded ends outwards, sometimes split or knapped to show their shiny inner surface. Clunch or chalk blocks appear in some places. Devonshire has its own material in the shape of cob or hardened mud and plaster, roofed invariably with thatch.

Roofing materials are as various as walls. The stone areas have their own slates such as the Collyweston slates of the Midlands and the Horsham slabs of West Sussex. In the north of England much thinner stone slates are found. Blue Welsh slates came into wide use in the nineteenth century.

These differences of material spring from the geology of each area, and largely determine its architectural style and character. They have a special value today, when even national styles are being replaced by a common international idiom. More than anything else, they give our historic towns the qualities for which they

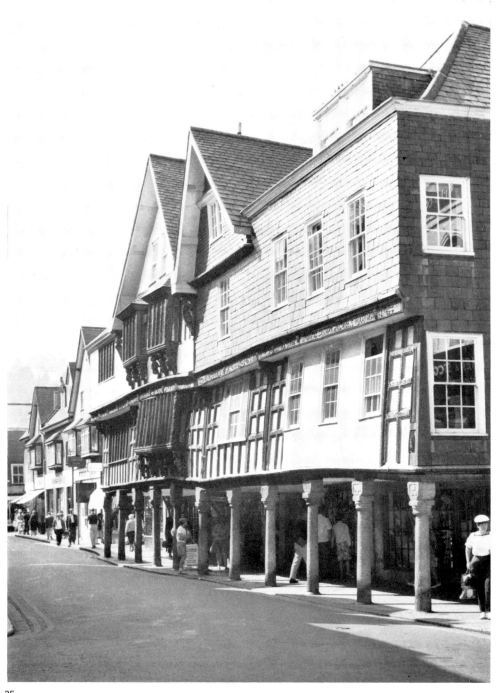

25

24   Church Hill, Midhurst

25   The Butterwalk, Dartmouth

are famous and which visitors come to admire.

Public concern that this rich and varied heritage should be protected has, over the years, given rise to many voluntary societies which enjoy wide support. The Society for the Protection of Ancient Buildings was founded in 1877 and the National Trust in 1895, to be followed in more recent times by the Georgian Group, the Victorian Society, the Civic Trust and numerous local societies.

Statutory machinery for preservation was introduced by the Town and Country Planning Act of 1944, the relevant pro- visions of which are now reproduced in the Town and Country Planning Act 1962. They provided for a comprehensive national inventory to be made, under the aegis of the Minister of Housing and Local Government, of all buildings of 'special architectural or historic interest' through- out the country.

Although the statutory lists are highly selective – they are confined to buildings of special interest – they cover a great

26 The Guildhall, Worcester

27 King's Stanley Mills, Stroud

28 Mozart's House, Ebury Street, London

29 Oriel Chambers, Walter Street, Liverpool

30

range and diversity of buildings. As well as the acknowledged gems (26), they include all the best buildings of each period, buildings eloquent of local history, buildings associated with famous men and women (28), buildings remarkable for technical innovation (27, 29), and a variety of structures of more particular interest (30). The lists so far issued cover over 100,000 buildings in all in England and Wales ; and the work is still going on.

These listed buildings must be the starting-point in any appraisal of claims to preservation. Between them they comprise the whole of our architectural tradition and all that is best in town buildings of the past. We cannot hope to preserve them all, for some must inevitably perish through age and decay, and a few to make way for necessary improvements. Many have been lost each year for these reasons, and the numbers that remain are gradually dwindling. It is all the more important that we should keep as many of those that are left as we can.

It is not only the individual buildings that matter : their settings may also be important. Visually as well as in other respects, a good building may be made or marred by what goes on around it (7). The protection of a listed building may therefore require the protection, and possibly the improvement, of its surroundings.

The historic centres of many old towns have a quality of their own which transcends the value of the individual buildings they contain. Here it is the whole composition that matters. Its virtue will lie not so much in particular architectural features, important though these may be, as in a compound of physical properties – the size and proportions of the buildings, their alignment and roof-lines, detailing, texture and colour.

30   The Jubilee Clock, Chester

Most of us are familiar with areas of this kind. They lie at the hearts of many of our ancient towns ; often of great beauty, they reflect the towns' history and are the clearest expression of their character and identity. If one were destroyed, the town would be immeasurably the poorer (31, 32).

In this case, what needs to be protected is the general shape and quality of the area, rather than each and every building within it. Some of the buildings may have strong claims to preservation in their own right, but the whole is more important than the separate parts.

There are still other qualities, besides fine buildings and historic areas, which may be of lasting value. These are more difficult to

31   The Market Place, Cirencester

32 The Market Place, Blandford Forum

31

32

33

34

define, but are none the less real. Perhaps
what we value most about the towns we
know and care for are those special
characteristics that in some way or other
give them their identity ; that set them
apart from other towns. It is a significant
fact that every town is different from the
rest : it is unthinkable, though not impossible, that there should be two alike.

These distinguishing features cannot all
be catalogued, for the ingredients of good
'townscape' are as diverse as those of
good landscape. They may be the result of
the town's physical setting : its aspect
when seen from outside (33), or views of
the country from within the town (34), or
the way in which town and country meet
(35).

33   Stamford

34   Kendal

35   Ludlow

35

36

Inside the town, changes of level, the historic street pattern, enclosed spaces and the scale of the buildings about them, sequences and sudden vistas, may all be distinctive elements which go to make up the town's identity (36, 38). Because these things are familiar, people tend to take them for granted ; but they notice their loss and are quick to protest when the damage has been done : when an interesting skyline is spoilt or a focal point obscured (37), or when the en-closure of a square is breached (39). It is better to be vigilant and to recognise such assets while they are still in our pos-session.

36   Whitby

37   Langham Place, London

38   Richmond, Yorkshire

39   Scarborough

38

37

39

3

A conservation policy

40

41

40   Pembroke Villas, Kensington

41   House in North East London

Hitherto preservation measures have concentrated chiefly on the protection of individual buildings. The tactics have been largely defensive, the defenders going into action only when a threat to a particular building has materialised. By then it is often too late : the building may already have been outflanked and isolated by new development, or it may have been neglected to such an extent that restoration or conversion to some new use is no longer possible.

If the position is not too badly compromised, the demolition of a building of special interest may be prevented by making a building preservation order. Many good buildings have been saved in this way, but a preservation order is a purely negative remedy. Its effect is to prohibit the demolition or substantial alteration of the building without the consent of the local authority ; but it does nothing to secure that it is kept in good repair. There are statutory powers for preventing historic buildings from being pulled down, but not — apart from the possibility of purchase by the local authority or the Ministry — for seeing that they are kept up. A building may be made the subject of a 'preservation' order only to collapse soon afterwards through structural decay. Several cases of this kind have occurred in recent years.

The real need is to ensure, so far as possible, that buildings of special architectural or historic value are properly maintained and cared for. Fortunately, most of them are. Where difficulties arise, they are usually economic : owners are unable or unwilling to spend money on repairs or restoration if the cost seems disproportionate to the probable return. In such cases grants to bridge the gap may be obtainable from the local authorities, from the Ministry of Housing and Local Government on the advice of the Historic Buildings Council (for buildings of outstanding importance), or possibly from some of the voluntary societies. But the amounts available necessarily fall far short of the potential demand.

Subsidies are in any case only a partial remedy ; they cannot be relied upon to provide for continued maintenance year in, year out. Money may be well spent initially on restoring or converting an old building which has fallen into disrepair or disuse, if it then becomes self-supporting, but there is a limit to what the community can afford to spend on old buildings that have no economic life of their own. Some are worth keeping for their beauty alone ; but the rest must earn their living in the world.

If it is to be effective, preservation policy must therefore reckon with the long-term economics of conserving historic buildings and areas, including the forces that contribute to their decline and, more positively, the conditions in which they are to live and prosper. It will recognise that historic buildings can seldom be considered in isolation, but only as part of a larger complex. A familiar illustration will bear this out. A small period house in a fashionable part of a large city will be in good condition and well-maintained (40). A similar building of the same age in a different quarter of the same town, beyond the railway goods yard and the gasworks, will be empty, and near-derelict (41). *The fate of historic buildings is largely determined by the quality of their environment.* No policy for preservation is likely to be more than marginally effective unless it recognises this and includes measures for securing the right environmental standards.

This is where preservation and planning have common ground. The conservation of good architecture and other qualities that enrich our towns needs to be planned, and planned with the same care and skill as are devoted to growth and redevelopment. During the last few years much attention has been paid to the tasks of urban renewal and the replanning of town centres, together with related questions such as housing densities, traffic circulation and car parking. Less thought has been given to the needs and problems of conservation. This gap urgently needs to be bridged. It would be

folly, while seeking to create a better urban environment, to cast away valuable assets we already possess. Systematic measures to conserve and make the best of these assets must be an essential element in planning for the future.

Planning preservation and change together is the surest way of avoiding conflict. It can provide opportunities of guiding the forces of change to assist conservation, by bringing new life to old areas and by diverting unwelcome pressures elsewhere.

4

Conservation in practice

Current planning practice puts more emphasis on conservation of the countryside than on conservation in towns. We have elaborate arrangements for the evaluation and classification of countryside, embracing national parks, areas of outstanding natural beauty, nature reserves, green belts and areas of high landscape value, each clearly defined and enjoying a special degree of protection. Up till now there has been nothing comparable for the towns, notwithstanding that ninety per cent of our population live in towns, that they embody historic and visual qualities of incalculable worth as well as the bulk of our architectural heritage, and that the threat to these things is much greater in towns than in the country. We have the statutory lists of buildings of special interest; but the lists themselves do not guarantee protection, and they deal with buildings in isolation rather than with 'townscape'.

The Civic Amenities Act of 1967 will now do something to redress the balance, by requiring local planning authorities to designate conservation areas – 'areas of special architectural or historic interest the character or appearance of which it is desirable to preserve or enhance', and it is the Government's policy to foster this approach.

The townscape survey

Comprehensive policies of conservation are needed for our towns as much as for the countryside, as an essential element in town planning. The need, as we have seen, is urgent. The first step for the planning authority to take should be a systematic survey of each town, covering its general character, shape and setting, and picking out the different features of visual or historic interest that are worth safeguarding. The net should be cast widely, to cover potential as well as actual assets, for most towns possess *latent* amenities which have not been fully realised (42, 43).

This townscape survey will include:

(a) buildings and groups of buildings of special architectural, historic or local interest. These will usually comprise all the buildings listed under section 32 of the Town and Country Planning Act 1962, but there may be others, especially 'Grade III' buildings.
(b) important street frontages or building lines, squares and spaces, where the general proportions, heights and alignment of buildings ought to be retained, even if some rebuilding takes place.
(c) areas of special character, as described earlier, which ought to be safeguarded as a whole because of their architectural and historic interest and their importance to the town's character and identity;
(d) other features of importance to the town as a whole: focal points, viewpoints and skylines, extending possibly to bits of landscape outside the town which should be kept open;
(e) 'opportunity areas', where there is potential scope for visual improvement; for example, a neglected river frontage.

There are many other possibilities, but the aim should be a general stock-taking of the visual assets of the town as a whole: to identify and plot all the features of the townscape which are worth keeping, or possibly improving, or which should influence the design of new development. The features in category (d) for example may provide the basis for a systematic high buildings policy; or they may be of special importance if large-scale expansion of the town is contemplated.

The results of the survey should be recorded in the form of an annotated map. This will be the foundation for the local planning authority's future conservation policy, and it will be an integral part of the framework upon which the future development of the town will be planned. In the process the survey material will have to be refined and tested against other planning proposals. Its compatibility with other plans for the town as a whole, particularly as regards road and

42   River front at Maidstone – opportunity area

43   River front at York – opportunity taken

44

town centre proposals, should be examined ; and if there are conflicts, adjustments – one way or the other – will need to be made. One point of cardinal importance needs to be stressed here. A conservation policy will never succeed if it is wholly negative or if it disregards the practical economics of conservation. It must allow for necessary change, and indeed should seek to guide it so that it will assist in the process of visual improvement. Hence the importance of integrating conservation with other planning proposals for the town.

Definition of conservation areas

One of the first steps will be to decide which areas of special character noted by the survey should be defined as conservation areas in accordance with section 1 of the Civic Amenities Act 1967. The statutory definition is 'areas of special architectural or historic interest the character or appearance of which it is desirable to preserve or enhance', and this will clearly cover a wide variety of areas. They may be large or small, ranging from whole town centres to squares, terraces and smaller groups of buildings. Listed buildings will usually be a prominent feature, but pleasant groups of other buildings, open spaces, trees, a historic street pattern or features of archaeological interest may also contribute to the special character of an area, and the presence of any of these, singly or in combination, will indicate places which should be considered for designation.

Each conservation area should be clearly defined, and public notice of designation has to be given. This should be accompanied, or followed as soon as possible, by a statement of the planning authority's proposals for the area.

Action in conservation areas

Once an area has been designated, the Civic Amenities Act makes it the duty of the responsible authorities to pay special

attention to the desirability of preserving or enhancing its character or appearance ; but more positive action will usually be needed. Conservation areas will often be in the centres of old towns, where the pressures for change and the threats to historic character are greatest. Here the pattern of the original streets and property boundaries may well persist, unchanged by rebuilding in the eighteenth and nineteenth centuries. Made for people on foot or horseback, the old pattern is now cracking and splitting under the strain of modern traffic.

Control of traffic

Excessive motor traffic is the bane of such areas. Apart from danger, noise and fumes, motor vehicles and especially parked cars are visually discordant and prevent people enjoying the beauty of buildings and places (44, 45). The vibration of heavy vehicles may damage old buildings. All these effects hasten the decline of the buildings themselves by degrading their environment.

In such areas the reduction of motor traffic will be the first aim of conservation. Total elimination may not be practicable, except perhaps as a long-term objective, so that immediate efforts will have to be concentrated on other methods, for example :
(a) re-routing through-traffic which has no business in the area ;
(b) one-way working and other measures to improve the circulation of the remaining traffic ;
(c) strict control of street parking, in the context of a general parking policy for the town ;
(d) restriction of new development likely to bring more traffic into the areas.

Control of development

From the outset every effort should be made to retain all the good buildings in a conservation area. The exteriors should be kept intact – or if possible restored where

44 45   'Motor vehicles are visually discordant'

the originals have been disfigured — although interior replanning or conversion may be necessary. It may be advisable for the local authority to make building preservation orders for all the listed buildings in the area to ensure that they have effective control over any proposals to demolish or alter them.

Where new development is permitted, the utmost care will be needed to see that the design is sympathetic to the context. This does not mean that design should be imitative, for good contemporary architecture can look well in any situation ; but that it should be properly related to its surroundings. But the emphasis should be on the restoration and rehabilitation of the original buildings whenever possible, rather than on building anew. Comprehensive redevelopment of large blocks will generally be ruled out.

A central conservation area may however be subject to many pressures, for which

accommodation must be found. New methods of retail trading are changing the outside as well as the inside of buildings. Stores and other big buildings — civic centres, libraries, bowling alleys — seek strategic sites which must be found somewhere. A supermarket needing wide spaces for shoppers and the display of goods takes up the space of three or four older shops. If it is built amongst them, the style of the street may be lost unless, as is generally quite possible, the design of the new building is adapted to fit the street (46).

If large-scale expansion of the town is envisaged it may be possible to build a new centre where big buildings can be grouped together away from the old. But in towns where total demand is not growing fast, if trade and activity are diverted away from the centre, shops there may close and buildings deteriorate. The only way will be to extend the centre. This, in fact, is a more hopeful way for most towns. Many shopping streets have some land that is not fully used behind the old shops. This land may allow room for a new extension of the shopping frontage, together with parking space, facing a pedestrian square or mall, sufficiently close to the old shops for continuity in pedestrian flows to be maintained, but sufficiently separate for the new large shop units not to overwhelm the small traditional shops. The point at which the facade of old shops is breached should be carefully chosen for its appearance as well as for making a convenient entrance to the vacant land.

The treatment of detail in a conservation area will also be important. Attention should be paid to the siting and design of street lights, road signs, electrical gear, litter-bins and all the paraphernalia of 'street furniture'. Much of it could perhaps be eliminated, given active collaboration between the different authorities concerned. Special attention should also be paid to the display of advertisements, and to the contribution which trees,

46   New store at Marlborough

shrubs, flowers and grass can make to the look of the place (47, 48).

Historic buildings

Few towns have so far worked out any positive strategy for the protection of their historic buildings. Most adopt a 'wait and see' attitude ; no action is taken until the local authority get notice of a proposal to demolish a building, accompanied usually by an application for permission to develop the site. By then it may be too late, if the building has been badly neglected or if it is already enveloped by new building.

Again, a positive approach to conservation is needed. The statutory lists already include buildings in Grades I and II, and the supplementary lists contain a third grade of buildings of lesser, but real, importance. The townscape survey will provide further information which will help in classifying buildings for the purposes of preservation. It will show which buildings are of the greatest importance to the town. It will also show which are obviously being well cared for by responsible owners, and, at the other end of the scale, those which clearly cannot be saved, either because of their poor physical condition or because they stand in the way of some essential development.

It is the buildings between these two extremes — those whose future is uncertain — which call for attention. This will entail a more detailed study to discover which buildings are in fact in danger, the nature of the danger in each case, and what steps could be taken to avert it. Some buildings will be found to be threatened by deterioration of their environment, in which case their future may depend upon what can be done to improve conditions by planning and traffic management. If this is impossible, wholesale redevelopment may be inevitable sooner or later.

47

48

47 48   Clutter — before and after treatment

In other cases the threat may arise simply from age and obsolescence, and the high cost of restoration or conversion to a new use. In such cases discussions should be held with the owners and the buildings should be surveyed, if necessary, to discover the amount of work and expenditure required. The local authority should then consider whether they would be justified in making a grant towards the cost. Both county and county district councils have power to make grants for this purpose under the Local Authorities (Historic Buildings) Act 1962, and quite a small contribution from each will often be enough to bridge the gap between the cost and what the owner is prepared to spend. If the building is of outstanding importance, the Historic Buildings Council can be approached for a grant. In several towns joint schemes have been worked out between the Council and the local authority under which both contribute to the maintenance and repair of important buildings.

In the last resort the demolition of a good building may be prevented by a building preservation order, and authorities should be prepared to make such orders wherever a convincing case is not made for demolition. And they should not be too easily convinced. Two points should be remembered : first that financial arguments used to support proposals for demolition are often suspect ; the fact that an old building is worth less to its owner as it stands than the new building that would take its place is in no way decisive. If it were, we could expect almost every historic building, whatever its importance, to be replaced by a block of offices or flats. Second, that the defects of the building are likely to be exaggerated, for a person who is intent on demolishing an old building will naturally be more inclined to harp on its faults than to sing its praise.

In fact, the restoration of old buildings is often financially rewarding, and many schemes of rehabilitation and conversion have been carried out with conspicuous success. Some examples are shown in the photographs (49-55).

52

53

54

55

Old houses into new

The rehabilitation of old residential areas which are basically sound may be particularly rewarding both for the sake of conservation and for the housing they provide. Groups or districts of old houses of character are part of the total stock of houses. Many of them provide good accommodation if they are kept in good repair : these the community needs. Many of them are near the town centre, and so long as they are lived in help to keep the centre alive.

Such areas are sometimes difficult to distinguish since they shade into others where houses are not worth keeping because they are basically unfit, or too large or too small, are not possible to convert to dwellings of the right size, or occupy land that could better serve other necessary purposes. The main questions to be taken into account are :
(1) can the houses be made to provide satisfactory accommodation ?
(2) will changes of use be necessary to ensure preservation ?
(3) will keeping such areas in residential use fit in with the rest of the town plan ?

Many old houses have occupants who appreciate their character and keep them in good repair. At the other extreme are those which cannot be made fit or which can be saved only if the council acquires them and rehabilitates or converts them for its own tenants. Between the two are houses whose owners can be encouraged, by grants or otherwise, to do the work — or compelled if the properties are tenanted.

The illustrations show two successful schemes of rehabilitation which have been carried out in London (51, 55).

49 50   20 Ship Street, Brecon, before and after treatment

52 53   Houses at Thurlaston, Leicestershire, before and after restoration

54   The Malthouse, Tidmarsh Lane, Oxford, converted to offices after fire damage

51   Portland Grove, Lambeth

55   Brandon Estate, Southwark

56

57

58

59

60

Both comprise pleasant early nineteenth century houses which were declining into slums and might easily have been overlooked and lost in the general clearance programmes.

Design in renewal

The conservation policy will influence both the siting and the design of new development in the town. It will affect the way the town grows, and help to define the changing relation of town to landscape; free in some directions, in others restricted to ensure that the outlook over hills or river valley is kept open. Within the town, it may be necessary to regulate the siting of high buildings to preserve a skyline, or the dominance of a church spire. Historic monuments such as city walls and castle, an ancient street pattern, or the grand design of period terraces and squares will all influence both the location and the quality of new buildings.

Architecture is a creative art; yet an old environment will always exert its own discipline upon new design. What sort of discipline must depend to some degree on the uniformity or diversity of the surrounding buildings and townscape. At one extreme is the consistent group of buildings – usually a terrace built as a single architectural entity; its unity is essential. If the character of the group is worth preserving at all, then alteration should be avoided and the rebuilding of individual units must copy the existing style and details as faithfully as possible (56).

Some groups, though not uniform, have a strong character running through them. The buildings may belong to the same period and be constructed of local materials. How different can the new building be? The illustrations provide some answers to this question (57–60).

56   Rebuilding in the Paragon, Bath
57   Balcombe Street, St. Marylebone, London
58   Lemon Street, Truro
59 60 Wimpole Street, London

61

62

At the other extreme is a mixed group : individual buildings of different periods and style, having little in common but their juxtaposition and the fact that each is good in itself and holds its own with the others. Here character may lie in slight changes in building line and corresponding variety in skyline, and the discipline may be to prevent a flattening out of these into a banal street scene restricted by the regular curb and the sweep of asphalt.

Often it is the building height that matters : the discipline needed is simply to maintain it. A drop from the high to the low skyline can ruin a street scene without bringing any credit to the building itself (61). But many streets in old towns have an intricate irregular skyline. Here the height of buildings may matter less than the variety of dormers, roofs and chimneys of the small units. The hard skyline of modern shops lined up with adjoining eaves looks monotonous and unfriendly (62).

The size, or rather the apparent size, of the unit is another key to character ; and this may pose problems where a large new store is to be inserted in an old shopping street. The architect may be required to break down a wide frontage to tally with neighbouring units.

Materials may suggest a discipline. New buildings will always stand out from the old, but the balance will be adjusted in time : cleaning or repainting the old may also put things right. Glass, and glazed materials, do not age : in an old street they should be played down. But contrast in materials, even in a uniform facade, is not necessarily bad. Decoration and detail should also be observed. A flat, bald insertion can disrupt a worthwhile continuity of heavily modelled facades. The proportion of window to wall is another important element. The rhythm of a street frontage may call for a measure of conformity : a sudden violent difference may shatter it (63).

61   Market Place, Henley-on-Thames (compare 63)

62   West Street, Horsham

63   Edmund Street, Birmingham (compare 61)

64

People, and the planning authorities they
elect, have the right to expect all these
points to be observed in the design of
new development where it is important
that the character of the place should be
respected and its architectural quality
maintained. For the architect, the discip-
lines imposed by environment should be
welcomed rather than resisted, for they
may offer a greater challenge than building freely on a virgin site. The results may
be more rewarding ; the design and
arrangement of the new buildings may
show up new qualities in the old, and both
may benefit from juxtaposition with one
another (64, 65).

64   Ripon Hall, Boars Hill, Oxford

65   Durham

65